For my first family,
and my second one - NR

For Emily, my favourite poet - EB

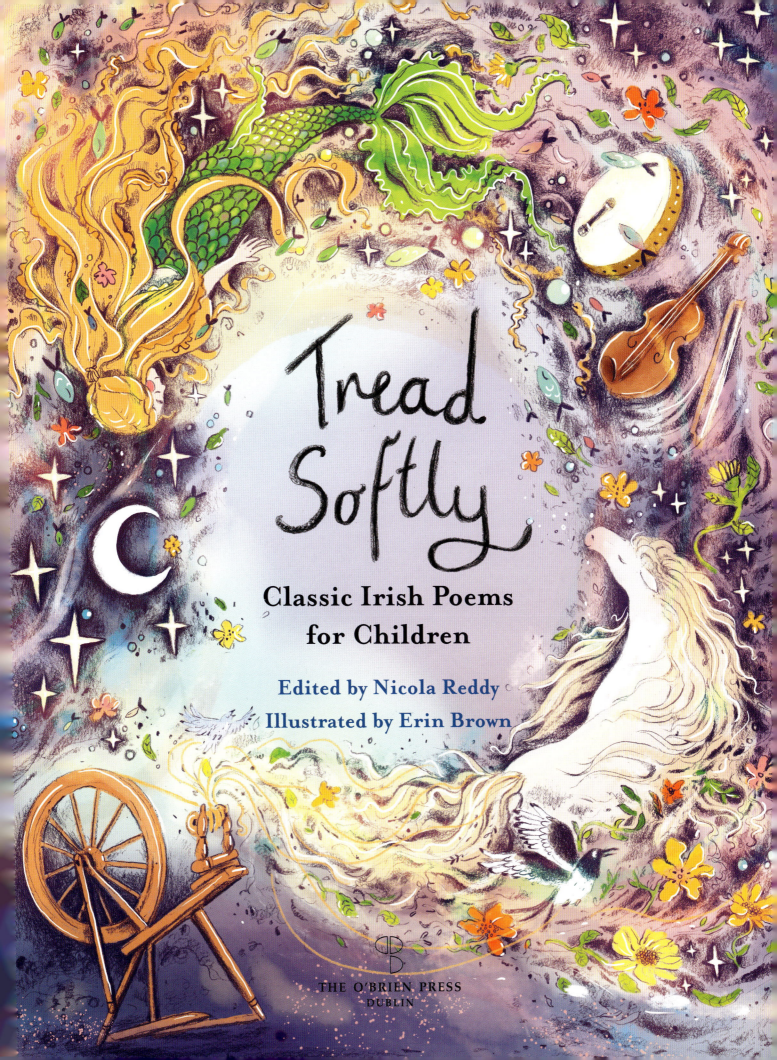

Introduction

My young daughter has always been fascinated by words. Whenever she comes across a new one, a furrow crosses her brow, followed by a little smile as she considers the potential of this tiny treasure. When she was learning to speak, one of our favourite books to read together was a giant collection of nursery rhymes. I knew many of them from my own childhood, but while reading them with a little one, I realised that they were full of strange, old-fashioned words. (Even I'm not quite sure what curds and whey are, never mind a tuffet.)

Watching her figure out these simple verses reminded me why the best poetry is so magical, for any of us, at any age. Even if at first it seems challenging or obscure, all it takes is a striking image or familiar idea, along with lovely rhythm and rhyme — and suddenly you're on the path to understanding and enjoying the whole.

Still, the most wonderful poems are also filled with mystery and nuance; they grow and change with the reader. The poems in this book, by some of Ireland's most celebrated writers, will feel a certain way when you read them first; they will feel different in years to come, transformed by your own knowledge and experiences; and different again if you choose to share them with someone you love.

Nicola Reddy

CONTENTS

'Aedh Wishes for the Cloths of Heaven' by W.B. Yeats — page 8

'Les Ballons' by Oscar Wilde — 10

'Lambs' by Katharine Tynan — 12

'On Snow: A Riddle' by Jonathan Swift — 13

'On the Beach at Fontana' by James Joyce — 14

'The Planter's Daughter' by Austin Clarke — 16

'The Heart of the Wood', anonymous, translated by Lady Augusta Gregory — 18

'Freedom' by George William (AE) Russell — 19

'Beg-Innish' by J.M. Synge — 20

'A Mayo Love Song' by Alice Milligan — 22

'The Fisherman' by Lady Jane Wilde — 24

'Home' by Francis Ledwidge — 26

'In Tír na nÓg' by Ethna Carbery — 28

'The Wayfarer' by Patrick Pearse — 32

'Echo' by Thomas Moore — 34

'I Am Raftery the Poet' by Antoine Ó Raifteirí, translated by Douglas Hyde — 36

'The Scholar and His Cat, Pangur Bán', anonymous, translated by Robin Flower — 38

'The Little Waves of Breffny' by Eva Gore-Booth — 40

'The Lake Isle of Innisfree' by W.B. Yeats — 42

'Aedh Wishes for the Cloths of Heaven'
W.B. Yeats

Had I the heavens' embroidered cloths,
Enwrought with golden and silver light,
The blue and the dim and the dark cloths
Of night and light and the half light,
I would spread the cloths under your feet:
But I, being poor, have only my dreams;
I have spread my dreams under your feet;
Tread softly because you tread on my dreams.

Aedh is the Celtic god of the underworld and was one of the Children of Lir.

'Les Ballons'
Oscar Wilde

Against these turbid turquoise skies
   The light and luminous balloons
   Dip and drift like satin moons
Drift like silken butterflies;

Reel with every windy gust,
   Rise and reel like dancing girls,
   Float like strange transparent pearls,
Fall and float like silver dust.

Now to the low leaves they cling,
   Each with coy fantastic pose,
   Each a petal of a rose
Straining at a gossamer string.

Then to the tall trees they climb,
   Like thin globes of amethyst,
   Wandering opals keeping tryst
With the rubies of the lime.

Oscar Wilde wrote this poem while watching children playing with their balloons in the Jardin des Tuileries in Paris.

'Lambs'
Katharine Tynan

He sleeps as a lamb sleeps,
Beside his mother.
Somewhere in yon blue deeps
His tender brother
Sleeps like a lamb and leaps.

He feeds as a lamb might,
Beside his mother.
Somewhere in fields of light
A lamb, his brother,
Feeds, and is clothed in white.

A riddle is like a puzzle in words. Jonathan Swift's gives the reader lots of clues to help them find the answer (snow!).

'On Snow: A Riddle'
Jonathan Swift

From Heaven I fall, though from earth I begin,

No lady alive can show such a skin.

I'm bright as an angel, and light as a feather,

But heavy and dark, when you squeeze me together.

Though candour and truth in my aspect I bear,

Yet many poor creatures I help to ensnare.

Though so much of Heaven appears in my make,

The foulest impressions I easily take.

My parent and I produce one another,

The mother the daughter, the daughter the mother.

'On the Beach at Fontana'
James Joyce

Wind whines and whines the shingle,
The crazy pierstakes groan;
A senile sea numbers each single
Slimesilvered stone.

From whining wind and colder
Grey sea I wrap him warm
And touch his trembling fineboned shoulder
And boyish arm.

Around us fear, descending
Darkness of fear above
And in my heart how deep unending
Ache of love!

James Joyce loved to combine words to make new ones, like 'pierstakes' and 'slimesilvered'.

'The Planter's Daughter'
Austin Clarke

When night stirred at sea,
And the fire brought a crowd in,
They say that her beauty
Was music in mouth
And few in the candlelight
Thought her too proud,
For the house of the planter
Is known by the trees.

Men that had seen her
Drank deep and were silent,
The women were speaking
Wherever she went —
As a bell that is rung
Or a wonder told shyly
And O she was the Sunday
In every week.

The 'planter' was the rich local landlord, whose house was hidden by rows of tall trees.

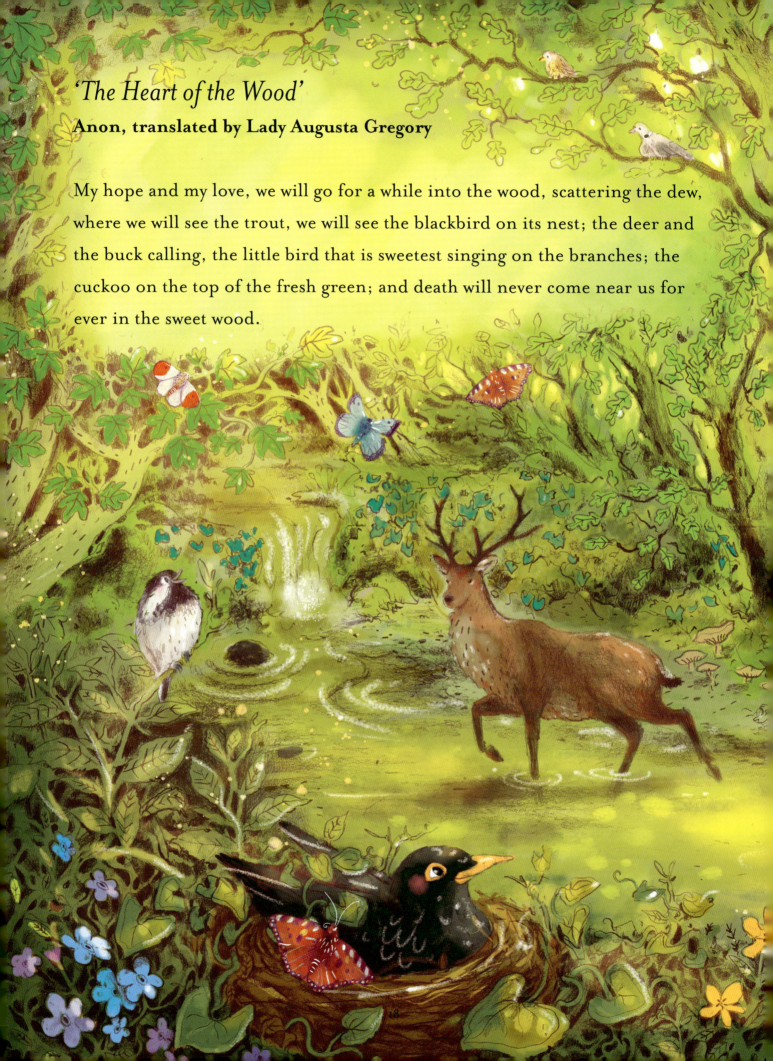

'The Heart of the Wood'
Anon, translated by Lady Augusta Gregory

My hope and my love, we will go for a while into the wood, scattering the dew, where we will see the trout, we will see the blackbird on its nest; the deer and the buck calling, the little bird that is sweetest singing on the branches; the cuckoo on the top of the fresh green; and death will never come near us for ever in the sweet wood.

'Freedom'
George William (AE) Russell

I will not follow you, my bird,
   I will not follow you.
I would not breathe a word, my bird,
   To bring thee here anew.

I love the free in thee, my bird,
   The lure of freedom drew;
The light you fly toward, my bird,
   I fly with thee unto.

And there we yet will meet, my bird,
   Though far I go from you
Where in the light outpoured, my bird,
   Are love and freedom too.

Many poets use images from nature to express their feelings. Here, animals and the forest are connected with love, peace and freedom.

'Beg-Innish'
J.M. Synge

Bring Kateen-beug and Maurya Jude
To dance in Beg-Innish,
And when the lads (they're in Dunquin)
Have sold their crabs and fish,
Wave fawny shawls and call them in,
And call the little girls who spin,
And seven weavers from Dunquin,
To dance in Beg-Innish.

I'll play you jigs, and Maurice Kean,
Where nets are laid to dry,
I've silken strings would draw a dance
From girls are lame or shy;
Four strings I've brought from Spain and France
To make your long men skip and prance,
Till stars look out to see the dance
Where nets are laid to dry.

We'll have no priest or peeler in
To dance in Beg-Innish;
But we'll have drink from M'riarty Jim
Rowed round while gannets fish,
A keg with porter to the brim,
That every lad may have his whim,
Till we up sails with M'riarty Jim
And sail from Beg-Innish.

J.M. Synge was a wealthy man from Dublin, but his plays and poems are mostly about ordinary life in tiny Irish towns and fishing villages.

'A Mayo Love Song'
Alice Milligan

It is far, and it is far,
To Connemara where you are,
To where its purple glens enfold you
As glooming heavens that hold a star.

But they shall shine, they yet shall shine,
Colleen, those eyes of yours on mine
Like stars that after eve assemble,
And tremble over the mountain line.

Though it be far, though it be far,
I'll journey over to where you are,
By grasslands green that lie between
And shining lakes at Mullingar.

And we shall be, and we shall be,
Oh, colleen lonely, beloved by me,
For evermore on a moor of Mayo
'Mid heather singing like the sea.

Alice Milligan travelled the country using plays and magic-lantern shows to teach Irish history.

'The Fisherman'
Lady Jane Wilde

I.

The water rushes — the water foams —
   A fisherman sat on the bank,
And calmly gazed on his flowing line,
   As it down in the deep wave sank,
The water rushes — the water foams —
   The bright waves part asunder,
And with wondering eyes he sees arise
   A nymph from the caverns under.

II.

She sprang to him — she sang to him —
   Ah! wherefore dost thou tempt
With thy deadly food, my bright-scaled brood
   From out their crystal element?
Could'st thou but know our joy below,
   Thou would'st leave the harsh, cold land,
And dwell in our caves 'neath the glittering waves,
   As lord of our sparkling band.

III.

See you not now the bright sun bow
   To gaze on his form here;
And the pale moon's face wears a softer grace
   In the depths of our silver sphere.
See the fleecy shroud of the azure cloud
   In the heaven beneath the sea;
And look at thine eyes, what a glory lies
   In their lustre. Come, look with me.

IV.

The water rushes — the water foams —
   The cool wave kiss'd his feet.
The maiden's eyes were like azure skies,
   And her voice was low and sweet.
She sung to him — she clung to him —
   O'er the glittering stream they lean;
Half drew she him, half sunk he in,
   And never more was seen.

Lady Jane Wilde, the mother of Oscar, wrote under the pen name Speranza — the Italian word for 'hope'.

'Home'
Francis Ledwidge

A burst of sudden wings at dawn,
Faint voices in a dreamy noon,
Evenings of mist and murmurings,
And nights with rainbows of the moon.

And through these things a wood-way dim,
And waters dim, and slow sheep seen
On uphill paths that wind away
Through summer sounds and harvest green.

This is a song a robin sang
This morning on a broken tree,
It was about the little fields
That call across the world to me.

Written in Belgium, July 1917

Francis Ledwidge died in World War I soon after writing this poem about his beloved County Meath.

'In Tír na nÓg'
Ethna Carbery

    In Tír na nÓg,
    In Tír na nÓg,
Summer and spring go hand in hand, and in the radiant weather
Brown autumn leaves and winter snow come floating down together.

    In Tír na nÓg,
    In Tír na nÓg,
The sagans sway this way and that; the twisted fern uncloses,
The quicken-berry hides its red above the tender roses.

In Tír na nÓg,
In Tír na nÓg,
The blackbird lilts; the robin chirps; the linnet wearies never,
They pipe to dancing feet of Sidhe and thus shall pipe for ever.

In Tír na nÓg,
In Tír na nÓg,
All in a drift of apple-blooms my true love there is roaming,
He will not come although I pray from dawning until gloaming.

In Tír na nÓg,
In Tír na nÓg,
The Sidhe desired my Heart's Delight, they lured him from my keeping,
He stepped within a fairy ring while all the world was sleeping.

In Tír na nÓg,
In Tír na nÓg,
He hath forgotten hill and glen where misty shadows gather,
The bleating of the mountain sheep, the cabin of his father.

In Tír na nÓg,
In Tír na nÓg,
He wanders in a happy dream thro' scented golden hours;
He flutes, to woo a fairy love, knee deep in fairy flowers.

In Tír na nÓg,
In Tír na nÓg,
No memory hath he of my face, no sorrow for my sorrow,
My flax is spun, my wheel is hushed, and so I wait the morrow.

In Irish mythology, Tír na nÓg is an island paradise where no one grows old.

'The Wayfarer'
Patrick Pearse

The beauty of the world hath made me sad,

This beauty that will pass;

Sometimes my heart hath shaken with great joy

To see a leaping squirrel in a tree,

Or a red lady-bird upon a stalk,

Or little rabbits in a field at evening,

Lit by a slanting sun,

Or some green hill where shadows drifted by

Some quiet hill where mountainy man hath sown

And soon would reap; near to the gate of Heaven;

Or children with bare feet upon the sands

Of some ebbed sea, or playing on the streets

Of little towns in Connacht,

Things young and happy.

And then my heart hath told me:

These will pass,

Will pass and change, will die and be no more,

Things bright and green, things young and happy;

And I have gone upon my way

Sorrowful.

Patrick Pearse was a writer, teacher and one of the leaders of the Easter Rising of 1916.

'Echo'
Thomas Moore

How sweet the answer Echo makes
   To Music at night,
When, roused by lute or horn, she wakes,
And far away, o'er lawns and lakes,
   Goes answering light.

Yet Love hath echoes truer far,
   And far more sweet,
Than e'er, beneath the moonlight's star,
Of horn, or lute, or soft guitar,
   The songs repeat.

'Tis when the sigh in youth sincere,
   And only then —
The sigh that's breathed for one to hear,
Is by that one, that only dear,
   Breathed back again!

In Greek mythology, Echo was a beautiful nymph who was only able to speak the last words spoken to her.

'I Am Raftery the Poet'
Antoine Ó Raifteirí, translated by Douglas Hyde

I am Raftery the poet,
   Full of hope and love,
With eyes that have no light,
   With gentleness that has no misery.

Going west upon my pilgrimage
   (Guided) by the light of my heart,
Feeble and tired,
   To the end of my road.

Behold me now,
   And my face to a wall,
A-playing music,
   Unto empty pockets.

Antoine Ó Raifteirí, who was blind since childhood, spent his life wandering the west of Ireland, singing songs and playing the fiddle.

'The Scholar and His Cat, Pangur Bán'
Anon, translated by Robin Flower

I and Pangur Bán, my cat,
'Tis a like task we are at;
Hunting mice is his delight,
Hunting words I sit all night.

Better far than praise of men
'Tis to sit with book and pen;
Pangur bears me no ill-will,
He too plies his simple skill.

'Tis a merry task to see
At our tasks how glad are we,
When at home we sit and find
Entertainment to our mind.

Oftentimes a mouse will stray
In the hero Pangur's way;
Oftentimes my keen thought set
Takes a meaning in its net.

'Gainst the wall he sets his eye
Full and fierce and sharp and sly;
'Gainst the wall of knowledge I
All my little wisdom try.

When a mouse darts from its den,
O! how glad is Pangur then;
O! what gladness do I prove
When I solve the doubts I love.

So in peace our task we ply,
Pangur Bán, my cat, and I;
In our arts we find our bliss,
I have mine, and he has his.

Practice every day has made
Pangur perfect in his trade;
I get wisdom day and night
Turning darkness into light.

This sweet poem was written in the margins of a manuscript by an Irish monk more than a thousand years ago.

'The Little Waves of Breffny'
Eva Gore-Booth

The grand road from the mountain goes shining to the sea,
And there is traffic in it and many a horse and cart,
But the little roads of Cloonagh are dearer far to me,
And the little roads of Cloonagh go rambling through my heart.

A great storm from the ocean goes shouting o'er the hill,
And there is glory in it and terror on the wind,
But the haunted air of twilight is very strange and still,
And the little winds of twilight are dearer to my mind.

The great waves of the Atlantic sweep storming on their way,
Shining green and silver with the hidden herring shoal,
But the Little Waves of Breffny have drenched my heart in spray,
And the Little Waves of Breffny go stumbling through my soul.

Eva Gore-Booth was born into an aristocratic family, but she spent her life campaigning for the rights of working women.

'The Lake Isle of Innisfree'
W.B. Yeats

I will arise and go now, and go to Innisfree,
    And a small cabin build there, of clay and wattles made;
Nine bean rows will I have there, a hive for the honey bee,
    And live alone in the bee-loud glade.

And I shall have some peace there, for peace comes dropping slow,
    Dropping from the veils of the morning to where the cricket sings;
There midnight's all a glimmer, and noon a purple glow,
    And evening full of the linnets' wings.

I will arise and go now, for always night and day
    I hear lake water lapping with low sounds by the shore;
While I stand on the roadway or on the pavements grey,
    I hear it in the deep heart's core.

W.B. Yeats was inspired to write this poem while walking down Fleet Street in London, where he was struck by a childhood memory of a beautiful lake in Sligo.

'Aedh Wishes for the Cloths of Heaven' by W.B. Yeats (1865–1939) from *The Wind Among the Reeds*, Elkin Mathews (London, 1899). 'Les Ballons' by Oscar Wilde (1854–1900) first published in *The Lady's Pictorial*, Christmas 1887. 'Lambs' by Katharine Tynan (1859–1931) from *Twenty-one Poems*, Dun Emer Press (Dublin, 1907). 'On Snow: A Riddle' by Jonathan Swift (1667–1745) from *The Poems of Jonathan Swift Vol II*, G. Bell and Sons, Ltd. (London, 1910). 'On the Beach at Fontana' by James Joyce (1882–1941), written in Trieste in 1914. First published in *Poetry: A Magazine of Verse,* November 1917; this version from *Pomes Penyeach*, Shakespeare and Company (Paris, 1927). 'The Planter's Daughter' by Austin Clarke (1896–1974) from *Pilgrimage and Other Poems*, Allen and Unwin (London, 1929); reprinted by kind permission of Carcanet Press, Manchester, UK. 'The Heart of the Wood' by Anon, translated by Lady Augusta Gregory (1852–1932) from *The Kiltartan Poetry Book: Poetic Translations from the Irish*, The Knickerbocker Press (New York, 1919). 'Freedom' by George William (AE) Russell (1867–1935) from *Collected Poems by AE*, Macmillan (London, 1913). 'Beg-Innish' by J.M. Synge (1871–1909) from *Poems and Translations,* Cuala Press (Dublin, 1909). 'A Mayo Love Song' by Alice Milligan (1865–1953) from *Hero Lays*, Maunsel & Co (Dublin, 1908). 'The Fisherman' by Lady Jane Wilde (1821–1896) from *Poems by Speranza*, M.H. Gill & Son (Dublin, 1864). 'Home' by Francis Ledwidge (1887–1917) from *Last Songs,* Herbert Jenkins Ltd. (London, 1918). 'In Tír na nÓg' by Anna MacManus / 'Ethna Carbery' (1864–1902) from *The Four Winds of Eirinn*, M.H. Gill & Son (Dublin, 1902). 'The Wayfarer' by Patrick Pearse (1879–1916) from *Collected works of Pádraic H. Pearse, Plays, Stories, Poems*, Phoenix Company (Dublin, 1917). 'Echo' by Thomas Moore (1779–1852) from *Irish Melodies,* Hurst, Rees, Orme and Brown (London, 1821). 'I Am Raftery the Poet' by Antoine Ó Raifteirí (1779–1835) from *Songs Ascribed to Raftery* by Douglas Hyde (1860–1949), Gill & Son (Dublin, 1903). 'The Scholar and His Cat, Pangur Bán' by Anon, translated by Robin Flower (1881–1946) from *The Poem-Book of the Gael: Translations from Irish Gaelic Poetry into English Poem and Verse*, selected and edited by Eleanor Hull, Chatto & Windus (London, 1912). 'The Little Waves of Breffny' by Eva Gore-Booth (1870–1926) from *The One and the Many*, Longmans, Green & Co (London, 1904). 'The Lake Isle of Innisfree' by W.B. Yeats (1865–1939) first published in the *National Observer*, December 1890.

First published in 2023 by
The O'Brien Press Ltd,
12 Terenure Road East, Rathgar,
Dublin 6, D06 HD27 Ireland.

Tel: +353 1 4923333; Fax: +353 1 4922777
E-mail: books@obrien.ie
Website: obrien.ie

The O'Brien Press is a member of Publishing Ireland
ISBN: 978-1-78849-411-3
Introduction and text selection © copyright Nicola Reddy, 2023
The moral rights of the author and illustrator have been
asserted.
Copyright for typesetting, layout, editing, design
© The O'Brien Press Ltd
Cover and internal design by Emma Byrne
Illustrated by Erin Brown

All rights reserved.

No part of this publication may be reproduced
or utilised in any form or by any means,
electronic or mechanical, including photocopying,
recording or in any information storage
and retrieval system, without permission
in writing from the publisher.
8 7 6 5 4 3 2 1
26 25 24 23

Printed and bound by Drukarnia Skleniarz, Poland.
The paper in this book is produced using pulp from
managed forests.

Published in

Acknowledgements

Thanks to Mum, my teacher; Dad, my hero; Annie and Hugo, my loves; and John, my everything. Thanks to the whole OBP team for their support from start to finish, especially Ivan and Kunak, Helen, Emma and Bex, and our brilliant sales, publicity and support folks. And to Michael, who is greatly missed. Thanks to Erin for her luminous artwork, without which we'd be nowhere at all.

NICOLA REDDY has worked in publishing for many years. By day, she edits books for readers of all ages, and by night, she loves to share her favourites with her two young kids. Originally from Waterford, she now lives in Dublin with her family and two very fluffy cats. This is her first book.

ERIN BROWN is a Northern Irish illustrator who lives and works on the beautiful island of Jersey. After she graduated from the University of Ulster with a bachelor's degree in Fine Art, a passion for stories and children's books took hold. She combines her love for hand-drawn lines and traditional techniques with the flexibility and freedom of adding colour digitally. When she's not working in her tiny studio, she can be found baking something overly sweet, exploring the forests and cliff paths of Jersey or down at the seashore, watching the tide roll in.